The Official Team GB and ParalympicsGB

TEAM GB

ParalympicsGB

Annual 2012

Andrew Arthur

CARLTON

The publishers would like to thank the following sources for their kind permission to reproduce the pictures in this book. The page numbers for each of the photographs are listed below, giving the page on which they appear in the book and any location indicator (C-centre. T-top. B-bottom, L-left, R-right)

Action Images: 60BC; /Jason Cairnduff: 19T; /Anthony Charlton/ODC: 20B; /David Grey/Reuters: 17TC; /Paul Harding: 14C, 25LB; /Jason Lee/Reuters: 59; /Brandon Malone: 56BL; /Steve Marcus/Reuters: 61TL; /Phil Noble/Reuters: 12TL, 61CT; /Jason O'Brien: 12BR; /Steve Paston: 21T; /Jason Reed/Reuters: 28BR; /Lee Smith: 6TL; /Aly Song/Reuters: 15L; /Bobby Yip/Reuters: 5, 35BR, 48BR

Getty Images: 49BR; /Peter Adams: 31B; /Brian Bahr: 27L; /Al Bello: 15TR, 29; /Daniel Berehulak: 21B, 57R; /Milos Bicanski: 34R; /Shaun Botterill: 12BL, 33B, 61BC; /Clive Brunskill: 10T, 47; /Geoff Caddick/AFP: 44R; /Central Press/Hulton Archive: 43T; /MN Chan: 35T; /Anthony Charlton/ODC: 8R; /Martin Child: 30BL; /China Photos: 9BR, 27TR, 40T, 41LT; /Ian Cumming: 31TL; /Carl de Souza/AFP: 16C, 22L; /Adrian Dennis/AFP: 46L; /Tom Dulat: 25R; /Don Emmert/AFP: 4R, 15TL; /Jonathan Ferrey: 22R, 22BR; /Frank Fife/AFP: 7, 60TC; /Stu Forster: 12TR, 13, 14R, 17BC; /Fox Photos: 30BR; /John Gichigi: 10B; /Paul Gilham: 36RT; /Cate Gillon: 49TR; /David Goddard: 37LB, 37B; /Alexander Hassenstein/Bongarts: 60TR; /Graham Hughes: 38TL; /Samir Hussein: 25TR; /Chris Jackson: 44L; /Nick Laham: 61TR; /Christopher Lee: 45T; /Bryn Lennon: 25L, 40BR, 50BL; /Feng Li: 41TL, 41LB, 49L; /London 2012 Ltd: 24TR, 25BL, 25LT; /Tom Lovelock/AFP: 25BR; /Clive Mason: 14BR, 36LT, 54, 55TL, 55R, 55BR; /Jamie McDonald: 37TR, 48L, 60C; /Darren McNamara/Allsport: 61TC; /Olivier Morin/AFP: 60TCR; /Dean Moutharopoulas: 17TR; /Marwan Naamani/AFP: 6BR; /Guang Niu: 26BC, 58L, 58B; /ODA: 36BL; /Adam

Pretty: 19BL, 26R, 28L, 49TL; /Gary M. Prior: 11T, 61BL; /David Rogers: 4L, 38BR; /Clive Rose: 38BL, 46BR, 61L; /Oil Scarff: 57B; /Jamie Squire: 15TC, 33T; /Ben Stansall/AFP: 16B; /Michael Steele: 6TR, 6BL, 60TCL; /Bob Thomas: 32L, 57T; /Topical Press Agency: 42-43BKG; /Ian Walton: 56TR; /Mark Wieland: 25TL; /WireImage: 60R; /Andrew Wong: 26L, 40BL

LOCOG: 17BR, 21L, 24L, 36LB

ODA: 8TL, 9T, 17C, 20C, 45C, 60BL

PA Photos: 14TC; /AP: 42R, 43B; /AP Photo/ODC: 36T; /Barry Batchelor: 41B; /Julien Behal: 18; /Lynne Cameron: 46R; /Anthony Charlton/ODC/AP: 45B; /Barry Coombs: 35BL; /Gareth Copley: 32R, 38TR, 39, 48R, 60TL; /Hou Deqiang/Landov: 23B; /Matt Dunham: 16R; /Zhang Duo/Landov: 58TR; /Christophe Ena/AP: 14BC; /Lo Ping Fai/Landov: 34BL; /John Giles: 32B, 61CB; /Anna Gowthorpe: 51BR; /Owen Humphreys: 37LT; /David Jones: 55BL; /Andrew Matthews: 36RB; /Andrew Milligan: 9L; /Rebecca Naden: 11B, 60BR; /Ian Nicholson: 24TL, 24B; /Phil Noble: 26BR, 61R; /Steve Parsons: 23T; /Nick Potts: 28R; /Martin Rickett: 8BC, 19BR; /Amy Sancetta/AP: 46BL; /John Stillwell: 24R; /Mark J Terrill/AP: 28BC; /Dave Thompson: 37TL; /Rui Vieira: 51R; /John Walton: 50R; /Kirsty Wigglesworth/AP: 14BR

Rex Features: /Kyriacou: 31R

Every effort has been made to acknowledge correctly and contact the source and/or copyright holder of each picture and Carlton Books Limited apologises for any unintentional errors or omissions that will be corrected in future editions of this book.

First published in 2011
Copyright © Carlton Books Limited 2011

Team GB lion's head logo ™ © British Olympic Association 2009.
All rights reserved.

Carlton Books Limited
20 Mortimer Street
London W1T 3JW

A CIP catalogue record for this book is available from the British Library

10 9 8 7 6 5 4 3 2 1

ISBN: 978-1-84732-366-8

Editor: Martin Corteel
Design Direction: Darren Jordan
Design: Simon Oliver
Picture Research: Paul Langan
Production: Maria Petalidou

Printed in Italy

Super sailor Ben Ainslie hopes to become a four-time Olympic gold medalist.

Tom Daley could become Team GB's youngest gold medal winner in 2012.

CONTENTS

Lee Pearson is a star member of the ParalympicsGB Equestrian team.

JESSICA ENNIS

HEPTATHLON HEROINE

One of the UK's brightest medal hopes at the London 2012 Games, Jessica Ennis is a talented all-round athlete who won gold at the 2009 World Championships in Berlin. She competes in the Heptathlon, a combined Track and Field event that includes the 100m hurdles, 200m, 800m, high jump, long jump, shot put and javelin.

4 AMAZING FACTS

1 Tipped to win a medal at the Beijing 2008 Games, Jessica suffered a double stress fracture in her right foot in a competition shortly before the Games opened and had to withdraw. Her treatment included sitting on a magnetic bed for an hour a day and spending 20 minutes with a special bone-healing medical machine. She was told the injury was career-threatening, but was back on the track less than 12 months later!

After missing Beijing 2008, Jessica is even more determined to win gold at London 2012

Jessica flew the flag proudly after her success at the 2010 European Championships

2 Jessica has saved her best performances for the biggest competitions. She won both the 2009 World Championships and 2010 European Championships Heptathlons, setting the year's best score. Her score of 6,823 points, set in Barcelona, was a personal best and a European Championships competition record by 45 points.

3 As a result of her foot injury in 2008, Jessica had to completely change her technique in the long jump event, and she now takes off from her left foot instead of her right. This is like growing up writing with your right hand and, suddenly, writing with your left and immediately being better.

The Heptathlon champion is seen as the best athlete in the world and Jessica is just that.

4 In addition to being the world's best heptathlete, Jessica is the world's best pentathlete too. In fact, her pentathlon feats may be even better than her Heptathlon. When she won the pentathlon gold medal at the Doha 2010 World Indoor Games, her score of 4,937 points set the World Indoor Championship, British and Commonwealth records. On day two of the event, she set personal bests in all three events, the shot put, long jump and 800m.

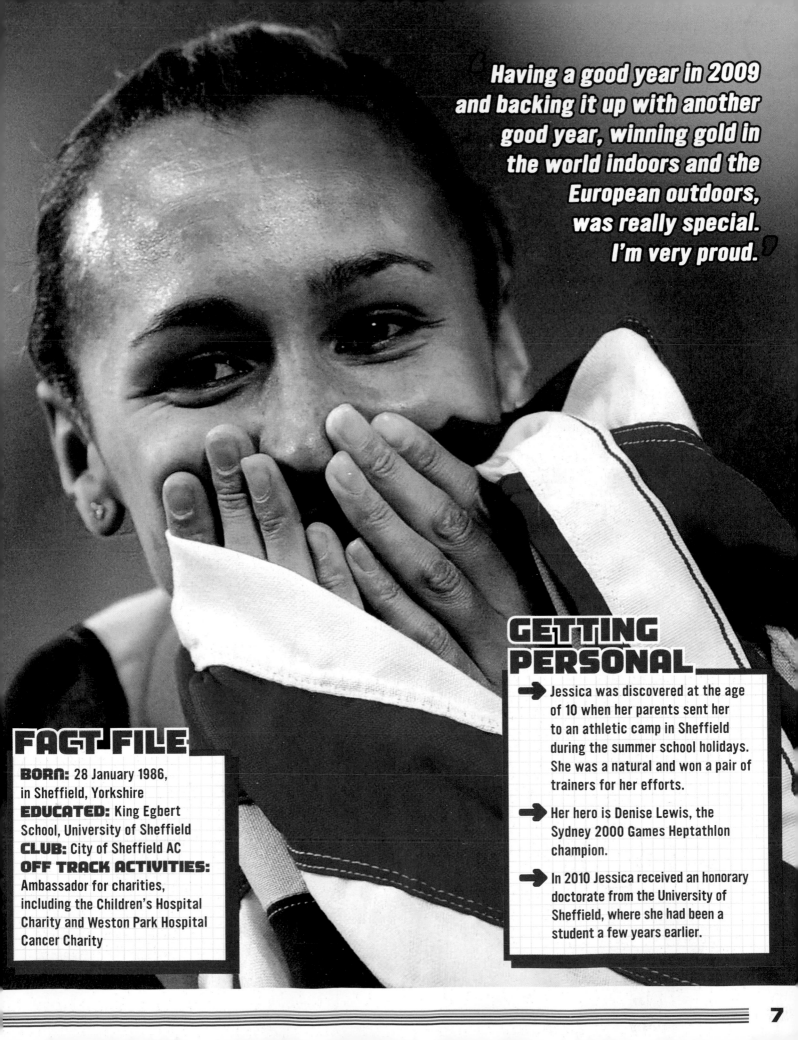

Having a good year in 2009 and backing it up with another good year, winning gold in the world indoors and the European outdoors, was really special. I'm very proud.

GETTING PERSONAL

➜ Jessica was discovered at the age of 10 when her parents sent her to an athletic camp in Sheffield during the summer school holidays. She was a natural and won a pair of trainers for her efforts.

➜ Her hero is Denise Lewis, the Sydney 2000 Games Heptathlon champion.

➜ In 2010 Jessica received an honorary doctorate from the University of Sheffield, where she had been a student a few years earlier.

FACT FILE

BORN: 28 January 1986, in Sheffield, Yorkshire
EDUCATED: King Egbert School, University of Sheffield
CLUB: City of Sheffield AC
OFF TRACK ACTIVITIES: Ambassador for charities, including the Children's Hospital Charity and Weston Park Hospital Cancer Charity

THE OLYMPIC PARK

WHAT'S ON AND WHERE AT THE GAMES (1)

The amazing 80,000-capacity Olympic Stadium and awesome Aquatics Centre aren't the only new sporting venues inside the Olympic Park in east London. Check out our brilliant guide to what else will be happening in Stratford during the London 2012 Games.

OLYMPIC STADIUM
VITAL INFO
WHERE IS IT? South of the Olympic Park
SPORTS: Athletics, Paralympic Athletics
SPOT THE STAR: Heptathlete Jessica Ennis is hotly tipped to grab gold for the UK inside the Olympic Stadium.
FAB FACT: The stadium is built on an island and five new bridges had to be constructed to connect it to the rest of the Olympic Park.
AFTER 2012? Premier League club West Ham United want the stadium as their new ground after the Games but have promised to keep the running track in place for athletics events.

OLYMPIC PARK IN NUMBERS

30 – The number of new bridges built in and around the Olympic Park

400 – Length in metres of the Olympic Park's BMX Track

2,000 – Number of new trees planted inside the Olympic Park

10,000 – Tonnes of steel used to build the Olympic Stadium

500,000 – Total number of spectators predicted to visit the Basketball Arena to watch the Basketball, Handball, Wheelchair Basketball and Wheelchair Rugby tournaments during the Games

Team GB's Luol Deng plays for the Chicago Bulls in the world's best basketball league, the NBA.

BASKETBALL ARENA
VITAL INFO
WHERE IS IT? North of the Olympic Park
SPORTS: Basketball, Handball, Wheelchair Basketball, Wheelchair Rugby
SPOT THE STAR: Chicago Bulls' legend Luol Deng will be the UK's main man in the Basketball.
FAB FACT: Organisers will have just 22 hours after the last Basketball match is played to transform the arena into a Handball venue.
AFTER 2012? The Basketball Arena will be dismantled and rebuilt elsewhere after the Games.

Shanaze Reade was in the BMX Cycling Final at Beijing 2008, but hopes for a gold at London 2012.

ETON MANOR
VITAL INFO
WHERE IS IT? North of the Olympic Park
SPORT: Wheelchair Tennis
SPOT THE STAR: Golden oldie Peter Norfolk is over 50 but he's the reigning Quad Singles champion.
FAB FACT: The Wheelchair Tennis courts are built on the old site of Eton Manor Sports' Club, a sports club set up nearly 100 years ago.
AFTER 2012? Eton Manor will become a top-class sports centre with 10 tennis courts, a hockey centre and five-a-side football pitches.

BMX TRACK
VITAL INFO
WHERE IS IT? North of the Olympic Park
SPORT: BMX Cycling
SPOT THE STAR: Triple world champion Shanaze Reade is favourite to land gold for Team GB.
FAB FACT: BMX riders will fly spectacularly over jumps, bumps and steep corners on the new track but blink and you'll miss it as each race lasts only 40 seconds.
AFTER 2012? The seats will be removed but the track will stay open to the public.

Peter Norfolk took gold in Wheelchair Tennis Quad Singles at Athens 2004 and Beijing 2008.

MEET THE COACHES

ATHLETICS CHIEF

NAME CHARLES VAN COMMENEE
TITLE HEAD COACH, UK ATHLETICS

■ Athletics is always one of the toughest sports at the Olympic Games but the determined Dutchman is desperate to guide Team GB to gold-medal glory on home soil in 2012.

➔ **Never let the athletes slack off**

➔ **Believe in the impossible**

■ Van Commenee is one of the strictest coaches in sport and he will never settle for second best. Expect to see a huge effort from every member of Team GB during London 2012.

■ His past record with the Dutch team and numerous individual athletes is awesome, so don't be surprised if we have a lot to celebrate in the Olympic Stadium in 2012.

ROWING GENIUS

NAME JURGEN GROBLER
TITLE HEAD COACH, BRITISH ROWING

■ Having personally coached gold-medal winning crews in each of the last five Olympic Games, the German-born coach is a true legend of the sport. His clever leadership skills and knack for pairing suitable rowers together has inspired Great Britain to huge success ever since he arrived in the UK in 1991.

➔ **Come up with new ideas to make the boat go faster**

➔ **Have a tactical Plan A and Plan B**

UK athletes will be raring to go at London 2012 thanks to the world-class coaches who have been busy training our medal hopefuls in the build-up to the Games. Check out our brilliant guide to four of the top coaches currently working with Team GB.

CYCLING MASTERMIND

NAME DAVID BRAILSFORD
TITLE PERFORMANCE DIRECTOR, BRITISH CYCLING

- The Welshman has helped transform British Cycling over the last decade and Team GB couldn't have a better coach to lead them into the London 2012 Games.

- Having inspired his team to 14 medals, including eight golds, at the Beijing 2008 Games, there is a big weight on his shoulders but his careful planning usually pays off.

→ **Study what you do wrong and put it right**

→ **Push yourself to the limit physically and mentally**

THE POOL PERFECTIONIST

NAME DENNIS PURSLEY
TITLE HEAD COACH, BRITISH SWIMMING

- The UK's top Swimming coach has pushed his stars to the limit in pursuit of medals at the Olympic Games, promising them that the more miles they swim in practice the easier it will be for them to win on the big day. Having won medals for Canada, Australia and his native USA in the past, he is a man who certainly knows what he's doing.

→ **Train hard and the races will come easy**

→ **Time your peak performances for the major championships**

PHILLIPS IDOWU

There are high hopes for Phillips Idowu to perform well at the London 2012 Games and after narrowly missing out on victory at the Beijing 2008 Games, the giant triple jumper will be targeting gold in front of his supporters in his hometown of London.

TRIPLE JUMP MAGICIAN

4 AMAZING FACTS

1 When Phillips won gold at the European Championships in Barcelona in 2010, he tied his son's teddy bear to his kit bag for good luck. 'You hear it "grrr" when I move the bag,' he said during the competition. 'Every time it goes off it reminds me of my daughter and my son, my girl at home and that regardless of how well or badly I do I am going home to a loving family.'

One of Phillips' heroes, Dennis Rodman, was also famous for his crazy hair

2 A silver medallist at the Manchester 2002 Commonwealth Games, Phillips claimed the first gold medal of his career four years later when he won the Commonwealth Games title in Melbourne.

Phillips will go into London 2012 as one of the gold medal favourites

3 The 1.97-metre Londoner had to be at his very best to be crowned World Champion in Berlin in 2009, producing a fantastic jump of 17.73m to beat Portuguese rival Nelson Evora and claim gold. It was a personal best for Phillips and the longest leap by any athlete in the world that year.

He set the best or second best Triple Jump distance every year since 2008

4 The Beijing 2008 Games ended in bitter disappointment for Phillips when he had to settle for a silver medal. He was in the lead after an impressive leap of 17.62m in the third round of the final only for Evora to jump just 5cm further in the fourth round and snatch the gold medal.

Phillips always seems to smile – except when he's actually jumping

FACT FILE

BORN: 30 December 1978 (Hackney, London)

EDUCATED: Raynes Foundation School, Brunel University

CLUB: Belgrave Harriers

CAREER HIGHLIGHTS: 2006 Commonwealth Games champion, 2007 European indoor champion, 2008 world indoor champion, 2008 Olympic Games silver medallist, 2009 world champion, 2010 European champion

GETTING PERSONAL

➡ Growing up in east London, Phillips was a talented Basketball and rugby player but decided to concentrate on Athletics and the Triple Jump. His sporting heroes were Hoops stars Michael Jordan and Dennis Rodman.

➡ Phillips has a very unusual way of relaxing before a big competition – two hours before he is due to jump he sits in his hotel room and pops the bubble wrap that he always packs. 'It helps you just space out,' he says. 'It's my form of meditation. I'll see if I can get through the whole sheet before competition.'

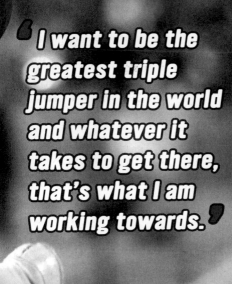

' *I want to be the greatest triple jumper in the world and whatever it takes to get there, that's what I am working towards.* '

GOLDEN MEMORIES

THE STORY OF THE UK'S TRIUMPHANT BEIJING 2008 OLYMPIC GAMES

The Beijing 2008 Olympic Games was the UK's most successful Games for a 100 years, with Team GB returning home with an incredible 19 gold medals. In total, our athletes won a fantastic 47 medals in China, leaving the UK fourth in the final medals table.

There was success for Team GB on the Track and in the Boxing ring but 16 of the team's 19 gold medals came in the Cycling, Swimming, Rowing and Sailing events. Cyclist Nicole Cooke began the gold rush when she won the Road Race on the third day of the Games. Track cyclist Sir Chris Hoy won three gold medals – in the Pursuit Sprint (beating fellow Team GB rider Jason Kenny in the final), Keirin and the Team Sprint. In the Pursuit events, Bradley Wiggins won two gold medals – Individual and Team – while Rebecca Romero won the women's Individual event. Rebecca Adlington was a double gold medallist in the Swimming pool, winning the 400m and 800m Freestyle. She set a new world record time for the 800m. Team GB also enjoyed a golden moment on the Athletics track when World Championship 400m winner Christine Ohuruogu became the Olympic champion. In the Boxing ring, James DeGale was the champion in the Middle Weight division. Sailor Ben Ainslie won his third Olympic gold medal in the Finn class, one of four Sailing triumphs for Team GB. In Rowing, Tom James, Peter Reed, Andy Triggs-Hodge and Steve Williams delivered in the Fours (4-) and there was also success for the men's Lightweight Double Sculls (2x) and Tim Brabants in the Kayak Single (K1) 1000m.

Top right: Christine Ohuruogu adds 400m Olympic gold to her world title.

Above: Yngling golden girls (l to r), Sarah Ayton, Sarah Webb and Pippa Wilson.

Above right: Victoria Pendleton with her Sprint gold medal.

Right: Nicole Cooke (middle) grabs the Road Race gold medal on the finish line.

Far right: Tim Brabants is a doctor but took 18 months out to return to Canoeing and won Kayak Single (K1) 1000m gold.

Top left: Sailor Ben Ainslie wins his third Olympic gold medal.

Top middle: Chris Hoy, Britain's first athlete in 100 years to win three golds at a Games.

Top right: Rebecca Adlington, double gold medallist in the Swimming pool.

Left: Continuing the Rowing tradition, Mark Hunter (left) and Zac Purchase.

GOLD MEDAL HAUL

ATHLETE	SPORT	EVENT
Rebecca Adlington	Swimming	400m Freestyle
Rebecca Adlington	Swimming	800m Freestyle
Ben Ainslie	Sailing	Finn Class
Sarah Ayton/Sarah Webb/Pippa Wilson	Sailing	Yngling Class
Tim Brabants	Canoeing	Kayak Single (K1) 1000m
Ed Clancy/Paul Manning/ Geraint Thomas/Bradley Wiggins	Cycling – Track	Team Pursuit
Nicole Cooke	Cycling – Road	Road Race (Mass Start)
James DeGale	Boxing	Middle Weight
Paul Goodison	Sailing	Laser Class
Chris Hoy	Cycling – Track	Keirin
Chris Hoy	Cycling – Track	Sprint
Chris Hoy/Jason Kenny/Jamie Staff	Cycling – Track	Team Sprint
Mark Hunter/Zac Purchase	Rowing	Lightweight Double Sculls (2x)
Tom James/Peter Reed/Andy Triggs-Hodge/Steve Williams	Rowing	Four without cox
Christine Ohuruogu	Athletics	400m
Victoria Pendleton	Cycling – Track	Sprint
Iain Percy/Andrew Simpson	Sailing	Star Class
Rebecca Romero	Cycling – Track	Individual Pursuit
Bradley Wiggins	Cycling – Track	Individual Pursuit

THE OLYMPIC PARK

WHAT'S ON AND WHERE AT THE GAMES ②

We've already checked out the Olympic Stadium, Basketball Arena, BMX Track and Eton Manor, but there are plenty more venues on show inside the Olympic Park. Here's the lowdown on the five other sites that will play a major part during the 2012 Games.

VELODROME
VITAL INFO
WHERE IS IT? North of the Olympic Park
SPORTS: Track Cycling, Paralympic Track Cycling
SPOT THE STAR: Team GB is packed with gold-medal hopes but none are more famous than Chris Hoy, who will be looking to add to the four gold medals he's won at previous Olympic Games.
FAB FACT: So much soil was dug up to create the Velodrome bowl that the earth would have filled nineteen 50m swimming pools.
AFTER 2012? The Velodrome will be a top Cycling venue and outside a new Mountain Bike riding course and Road Cycling circuit will be built; it will be known as the VeloPark.

Sir Chris Hoy, the first knight of the track, won three gold medals at Beijing 2008.

HANDBALL ARENA
VITAL INFO
WHERE IS IT? West of the Olympic Park
SPORTS: Handball, Modern Pentathlon (fencing), Goalball
SPOT THE STAR: Teenager Georgina Bullen will be crucial to ParalympicsGB's hopes in the action-packed sport of Goalball.
FAB FACT: The outside of this state-of-the-art venue is covered in special metal sheeting, made from recycled copper, and it will change colour as it gets older.
AFTER 2012? The venue will be transformed into a health and fitness club open to the public, with basketball, handball, badminton, boxing, martial arts, netball, table tennis, wheelchair rugby and volleyball all on offer.

AQUATICS CENTRE

VITAL INFO

WHERE IS IT? South east of the Olympic Park

SPORTS: Diving, Swimming, Synchronised Swimming, Modern Pentathlon (Swimming), Paralympic Swimming

SPOT THE STAR: Rebecca Adlington was amazing in the pool at Beijing 2008 and will be aiming for gold again in London.

FAB FACT: With its amazing curved roof, the Aquatics Centre will be the first venue many visitors see when they enter the Olympic Park.

AFTER 2012? The Centre will be transformed into a facility for the local community, clubs and schools, as well as elite swimmers.

WATER POLO ARENA

VITAL INFO

WHERE IS IT? South east of the Olympic Park

SPORTS: Water Polo

SPOT THE STAR: GB star Sean Ryder has been playing in Romania for the last few years to get himself into top shape for 2012.

FAB FACT: The Arena has a distinctive silver wrap and inflatable ribbed roof made from recyclable plastic.

AFTER 2012? The Arena will be taken down but the plan is to reuse or relocate parts of it to other areas of the UK.

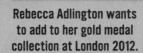

Rebecca Adlington wants to add to her gold medal collection at London 2012.

HOCKEY CENTRE

VITAL INFO

WHERE IS IT? South of the Olympic Park

SPORTS: Hockey, Paralympic 5-a-side Football, Paralympic 7-a-side Football

SPOT THE STAR: Beth Storry is Team GB's Hockey goalkeeper and is rated as one of the world's best.

FAB FACT: It cost a massive £19 million to build the Olympic Hockey Centre.

AFTER 2012? The Centre will move to the north of the Olympic Park to become part of the facilities in the area known as Eton Manor.

Hockey goalie Beth Storry is a hard woman to beat. Can she win gold at the Hockey Centre?

ELLIE SIMMONDS

SWIMMING PHENOMENON

Since bursting on to the international scene as an unknown 13-year-old with two sensational swimming gold medals at the Beijing 2008 Paralympic Games, Ellie Simmonds has continued to capture the hearts and minds of the British public. The teenager is truly in a league of her own as a swimmer.

4 AMAZING FACTS

1 Inside Beijing's stylish Water Cube swimming venue, Ellie became the UK's youngest ever individual gold medallist in either the Paralympic or Olympic Games. With just 25 metres to go she was in fourth place but an amazing finish saw her storm to an astonishing victory in the 100m Freestyle event.

GETTING PERSONAL

➜ In 2009 Ellie became the youngest ever team captain on hit TV game show *All Star Family Fortunes*. Competing with her aunt, cousin, brother and coach, Ellie lost out to Olympic champion Denise Lewis and her family but still did well enough to win a massive £1,520 for her chosen charity.

➜ She might only be 1.23m tall, but Ellie didn't let that stand in her way of auditioning for the part of a 'giant' in one of her school plays. Her determination paid off and she got the role.

2 In February 2009 Ellie became the youngest person ever to be awarded an MBE by Her Majesty the Queen. To top off a fantastic day at Buckingham Palace she was joined by her coach Billy Pie, who was also given the honour. He had kept it a secret from Ellie until the last minute.

Ellie joined the Beijing 2008 gold rush at the age of just 13.

'The motto at my training pool is: "Coming second is not an option."'

FACT FILE

BORN: 11 November 1994 (West Midlands)
EDUCATED: Olfcha Comprehensive (Swansea)
TEAM: Swansea Stingrays Disability Swimming Club
CAREER HIGHLIGHTS: 2008 Paralympics gold (400m Freestyle), 2008 Paralympics gold (100m Freestyle), 2008 BBC Young Sports Personality of the Year, 2009 European Championships five gold medals, 2009 World Championships six gold medals, 2010 Paralympics World Cup gold (200m Individual Relay), 2010 World Championships four gold medals, 2010 World Championships two world records

Ellie's flying finish brought her two gold medals at Beijing 2008.

4 On her return from the Beijing 2008 Paralympic Games, she was given a heroine's welcome by the 2,000 pupils at her school in Swansea who all cheered her as she turned up for lessons. Ellie was given a giant cake in the shape of a gold medal and everyone was given a half day off to celebrate.

3 Ellie moved from the West Midlands to Wales with her mum at the age of 13 so that she could train with her coach in a 50m pool on a daily basis. She has nine gruelling two-hour sessions a week and somehow also finds time to do her schoolwork.

Although born in Walsall, England, Ellie goes to school in Swansea, Wales.

VILLAGE PEOPLE

INSIDE THE OLYMPIC VILLAGE

More than 17,000 athletes and officials from all over the world will live together inside the Olympic Village in the Olympic Park as they take part in the greatest show on earth. As well as staying in brand–new, specially built apartments that have been equipped with all the latest mod cons, the athletes will also be able to visit the Park's brilliant Village Plaza, where they can hang out with their friends and family.

THE ROOMS

Each apartment in the Olympic Village will have comfy new beds and there will also be extra-long ones to make sure the taller athletes still get a good night's sleep. Wi-Fi internet will be available inside the rooms and just to make sure the athletes don't get homesick, they can have newspapers from their home country delivered right to their front door.

Right: The Olympic Park is a place to watch the world go by. Below: The world's media will be have a place to work 24/7.

COVERING THE GAMES

The Park's new International Broadcast Centre and Main Press Centre will be open 24 hours a day so that the world's media will be able to cover the London 2012 Games around the clock.

More than 20,000 broadcasters, journalists and photographers are expected to use the two centres during the Games. They will be covering London 2012 for an estimated global audience of four billion people. The only way to get inside the media zone will be with a special press badge.

Around 50,000 meals will be served each day to members of the media. A 200m long high street will connect the International Broadcast Centre and Main Press Centre and will have shops, banks, travel agents and even a post office.

GETTING AROUND

The Olympic Stadium will stage many of the Games events but if athletes need to cross the city for their event, they can be in Central London in just seven minutes by using the high-speed Javelin® train, running between St Pancras and Stratford International. The service will be able to carry up to 25,000 passengers every hour.

Top: Stratford will become an even busier transport hub. Left: There is much to see and do in peace and quiet close to the action. Below: The high-speed Javelin® train.

TIME TO UNWIND

If the athletes get bored sitting in their rooms watching TV or chatting to mates on Twitter and Facebook, they'll be able to watch a film at the Village cinema, watch the Games on a giant screen inside the Park, have a relaxing massage at the health spa or unwind with a game of table football in the on-site games room.

STAYING IN SHAPE

The Park's gym will come in handy for athletes looking to pump some iron but there are also a number of other hi-tech training facilities at Eton Manor on the north side of the Park to make sure the thousands of competitors will be raring to go for their events.

CHRIS HOY

KING OF THE VELODROME

Chris Hoy is an awesome, medal–winning machine and along with his four Olympic Games Cycling gold medals, the flying Scotsman has won an amazing 10 World Championship titles. He was crowned Olympic champion for the first time at Athens 2004, but hit the headlines four years later when he landed a record–breaking gold medal hat–trick at Beijing 2008.

4 AMAZING FACTS

1 Chris won gold in three different events at the 2008 Beijing Games and was champion in both the Sprint and Team Sprint events. His other gold came in the Keirin event – an exciting race where the cyclists all follow behind a small motorcycle for the first five-and-a-half laps in the Velodrome before battling it out with each over the final two-and-a-half laps.

Sir Chris was first to test the track at London 2012's Velodrome.

2 At Beijing 2008, he became the first Briton for 100 years to win three gold medals at a single Olympic Games and later that year he was voted BBC Sports Personality of the Year. In 2009, he became Sir Chris after being awarded a Knighthood by the Queen.

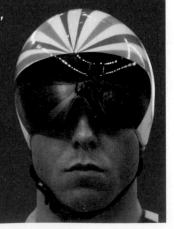

FACT FILE

BORN: 23 March, 1976 (Edinburgh, Scotland)
EDUCATED: George Watson's College, University of Edinburgh
TEAM: Team Sky+ HD
CAREER HIGHLIGHTS: Sydney 2000 Games silver medal (Team Sprint), Athens 2004 Games gold medal (1km Time Trial), Beijing 2008 Games gold medals (Sprint, Team Sprint and Keirin), 10 World Championships

'The opportunity to race in front of a home crowd at an Olympics is a once in a lifetime experience and I'm really looking forward to that.'

GETTING PERSONAL

➤ Before he became a star cyclist in the Velodrome, Chris raced BMXs until he was 14 years old and was a junior Scottish champion.

➤ After winning his amazing three gold medals at Beijing 2008, British Airways decided to name one of their jumbo jets after the Scotsman to celebrate his Olympic success.

3 The first Olympic medal of his brilliant career came at the Sydney 2000 Games when he, Craig Maclean and Jason Queally won the silver in the Team Sprint.

4 Chris is also a World Championship legend and three different times he has won two gold medals at the championships. He claimed his first golden double in Denmark in 2002 and repeated the trick in 2007 in Spain. His most recent two-gold haul was in 2008 in Manchester.

BEYOND THE PARK
LONDON'S OTHER VENUES

The Olympic Park in Stratford isn't the only place in London where you can catch some Games action. Here's a guide to the other venues in the capital that are set to play host to some of the world's greatest athletes in 2012.

EARLS COURT

DISTANCE: 6.1 miles from the Olympic Park
SPORT: Volleyball
DID YOU KNOW? You could fit four huge Boeing 747 jumbo jets inside Earls Court Two, the second of the centre's massive halls.

EXCEL LONDON

DISTANCE: 3.9 miles from the Olympic Park
SPORTS: Boxing, Fencing, Judo, Table Tennis, Taekwondo, Weightlifting, Wrestling, Boccia, Paralympic Judo, Paralympic Table Tennis, Powerlifting, Volleyball (Sitting), Wheelchair Fencing
DID YOU KNOW? Some of the *X Factor* and *Britain's Got Talent* live auditions take place inside the ExCel.

GREENWICH PARK

DISTANCE: 4.2 miles from the Olympic Park
SPORTS: Equestrian (Jumping, Dressage and Eventing), Paralympic Equestrian, Modern Pentathlon (riding and combined event)
DID YOU KNOW? Although located in a big city, the Park is home to a small herd of wild deer.

HAMPTON COURT PALACE

DISTANCE: 15.8 miles from the Olympic Park
SPORTS: Cycling – Road
DID YOU KNOW? The Mall begins in front of Buckingham Palace and will be part of The Queen's Diamond Jubilee celebrations in 2012.

HORSE GUARDS PARADE
DISTANCE: 3.6 miles from the Olympic Park
SPORT: Beach Volleyball
DID YOU KNOW? Prime Minister David Cameron's back garden at 10 Downing Street is joined to Horse Guards Parade.

HYDE PARK

DISTANCE: 5.2 miles from the Olympic Park
SPORTS: Triathlon, Marathon Swimming
DID YOU KNOW? The Park is home to the annual Wireless Festival, which featured the Black Eyed Peas, Pulp and Chemical Brothers in 2011.

LORD'S CRICKET GROUND

DISTANCE: 5.8 miles from the Olympic Park
SPORT: Archery
DID YOU KNOW? Lord's is home to the oldest sports museum in the world, where the famous Ashes urn is on display.

THE MALL

DISTANCE: 3.6 miles from the Olympic Park
SPORTS: Marathon, Race Walk, Paralympic Marathon, Cycling – Road
DID YOU KNOW? The Mall begins in front of Buckingham Palace and will be part of The Queen's Diamond Jubilee celebrations in 2012 – just 36 days before the Games start.

NORTH GREENWICH ARENA

DISTANCE: 4.2 miles from the Olympic Park
SPORTS: Gymnastics – Artistic, Gymnastics – Trampoline, Basketball, Wheelchair Basketball
DID YOU KNOW? In March 2011, the Arena was the venue for a basketball clash between New Jersey Nets and Toronto Raptors – the first ever NBA game played in Europe.

THE ROYAL ARTILLERY BARRACKS

DISTANCE: 6.6 miles from the Olympic Park
SPORTS: Shooting, Paralympic Archery, Paralympic Shooting
DID YOU KNOW? It cost £18 million to build the new Shooting hall at the Barracks.

WEMBLEY ARENA

DISTANCE: 9.9 miles from the Olympic Park
SPORTS: Badminton, Gymnastics – Rhythmic
DID YOU KNOW? The Arena once boasted a swimming pool, which was used during the London 1948 Olympic Games.

WIMBLEDON

DISTANCE: 9.6 miles from the Olympic Park
SPORT: Tennis
DID YOU KNOW?
Centre Court at Wimbledon is the most famous tennis arena in the world, but there are 18 other courts used for the Championships.

WEMBLEY STADIUM

CAPACITY: 9.9 miles from the Olympic Park
SPORT: Football
DID YOU KNOW? The famous arch at Wembley Stadium soars more than 133m into the sky.

GO FIGURE

8 – Length in millimetres of the grass on Wimbledon's Centre Court
12 – Number of football pitches that would fit inside the North Greenwich Arena
798 – Millions of pounds it cost the Football Association to build the new Wembley Stadium
200,000 – Estimated number of people who crammed into Hyde Park for the Live 8 concert in 2005
212,000 – Tonnes of concrete used to build Wembley Stadium

PARALYMPIC SPORTS

The London 2012 Paralympic Games will attract more than 4,000 athletes from around the world to compete for medals in 20 different sports. Many are modified from able-bodied sports while others, such as Boccia and Goalball, were specially created for the athletes with disability. Here is a guide.

John McFall was a 100m bronze medallist at the Beijing 2008 Paralympic Games.

ATHLETICS
Staged at the Olympic Stadium in east London, there will be Track races from 100m to 5000m, and jumping and throwing events.

SWIMMING
One of the most popular sports at the Paralympic Games, Swimming will see 600 men and women competing for 148 gold medals at London 2012.

FOOTBALL 5-A-SIDE
Fast, action-packed and unpredictable, it's for visually impaired players. Everyone except the goalkeepers are blindfolded and there is a noise-making device inside the ball.

VOLLEYBALL (SITTING)
It's just like able-bodied volleyball except all the competitors must sit on the floor, always keeping a part of the body between the buttocks and the shoulders in contact with the floor when playing or attempting to play the ball.

SHOOTING
Using either rifles or pistols, Paralympic competitors shoot from distances of 10, 25 and 50 metres from a standing, kneeling or prone position.
DID YOU KNOW? An average shooting competition usually lasts between 75 minutes and two hours.

BOCCIA
Boccia (pronounced Botch-ah) is similar to bowls and sees competitors throw leather balls at a white target ball from a seated position.

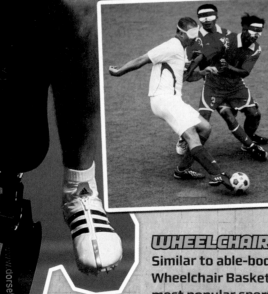

GOALBALL
Think football but blindfolded players throw rather than kick the ball. There's total silence during games so that the players can hear the bells inside the ball.

WHEELCHAIR BASKETBALL
Similar to able-bodied basketball, Wheelchair Basketball is one of the most popular sports in the Paralympic Games. Worldwide, there are around 25,000 players.

POWERLIFTING

Divided into different weight categories, athletes test their strength lying on their backs and bench-pressing enormous weights.
DID YOU KNOW? Top powerlifters can lift four times their own body weight.

WHEELCHAIR RUGBY

A combination of rugby, handball and basketball, Wheelchair Rugby is played on a basketball court using a volleyball.
DID YOU KNOW? The game is so tough it was originally called Murderball.

Murderball, a 2005 documentary on Wheelchair Rugby, was nominated for an Oscar.

GET THE KNOWLEDGE

SPORT	WHERE	WHEN	GOLD MEDALS AVAILABLE	FIRST IN GAMES
Paralympic Archery	The Royal Artillery Barracks	30 Aug–5 Sept	9	1960
Paralympic Athletics	Olympic Stadium	31 Aug–9 Sept	170	1960
Boccia	ExCeL	2–8 Sept	7	1984
Paralympic Cycling – Road	Brands Hatch	5–8 Sept	32	1984
Paralympic Cycling – Track	Velodrome	30 Aug–2 Sept	18	1996
Paralympic Equestrian	Greenwich Park	30 Aug–4 Sept	11	1984
Football 5-a-side	Hockey Centre	31 Aug–8 Sept	1	2004
Football 7-a-side	Hockey Centre	1–9 Sept	1	1984
Goalball	Handball Arena	30 Aug–7 Sept	2	1976
Paralympic Judo	ExCeL	30 Aug–1 Sept	13	1988
Powerlifting	ExCeL	30 Aug–5 Sept	20	1964
Paralympic Rowing	Eton Dorney	31 Aug–2 Sept	4	2008
Paralympic Sailing	Weymouth and Portland	1–6 Sept	3	2000
Paralympic Swimming	Aquatics Centre	30 Aug–8 Sept	148	1960
Paralympic Table Tennis	ExCeL	30 Aug–8 Sept	29	1960
Volleyball (Sitting)	ExCeL	30 Aug–8 Sept	2	1980
Wheelchair Basketball	North Greenwich Arena and Basketball Arena	30 Aug–8 Sept	2	1960
Wheelchair Fencing	ExCeL	4–8 Sept	12	1960
Wheelchair Rugby	Basketball Arena	5–9 Sept	1	2000
Wheelchair Tennis	Eton Manor	1–8 Sept	6	1992

REBECCA ADLINGTON

QUEEN OF THE POOL

Rebecca Adlington became Team GB's first female Olympic swimming champion for 48 years when she took the gold medal in the 400m Freestyle at the Beijing 2008 Games. Five days later she smashed the world record in the 800m Freestyle, becoming the first UK swimmer to win two golds at one Games for 100 years.

4 AMAZING FACTS

1 When Rebecca won her record-breaking women's 800m Freestyle gold medal in Beijing, she broke the world record that had been set by American Janet Evans. The record had stood for 19 years but Rebecca smashed it by two full seconds on her way to the title.

Rebecca was six months old when the old 800m world record was set.

2 Rebecca's hometown of Mansfield was so proud of her fantastic achievements at the Beijing 2008 Olympic Games that the local council decided to rename the pool where she had learnt to swim as a child in her honour. So if you are ever in Mansfield, you can now take a dip at the Rebecca Adlington Swimming Centre.

Rebecca collects designer shoes as well as gold medals.

3 Rebecca began swimming when she was just four years old and was taking part in competitive races by the age of 10. Just two years later she got her hands on the first gold medals of her glittering career when she won the 200m and 800m Freestyle at the National Age Group Championships.

In the 400m Freestyle, Rebecca's team-mate Jo Jackson won bronze.

4 The first major success of her senior career came in 2008 when Rebecca claimed gold in the 800m Freestyle at the World Championship Short Course competition in Manchester. She has since won two gold medals, representing England, at the Delhi 2010 Commonwealth Games.

Rebecca has already won six Swimming gold medals in her senior career.

FACT FILE

BORN: 17 February 1989
(Mansfield, Nottinghamshire)
EDUCATED: The Brunts School
CLUB: Nova Centurion
CAREER HIGHLIGHTS:
2008 world short course champion
(800m Freestyle), 2008 Olympic
champion (400m Freestyle, 800m
Freestyle), 2010 European long
course champion (400m Freestyle),
2010 Commonwealth champion
(400m Freestyle, 800m Freestyle)

'I train ten times a week in the pool, each session lasts two hours. Additionally I spend one hour a day doing dry land work either running or gym work.'

GETTING PERSONAL

→ Rebecca is a big fan of theme parks. Her favourite holiday destination is America because she thinks that's where all the best parks, such as Disney World, are.

→ Rebecca follows a strict diet when she is training for a major competition, but when she's allowed a treat her favourite meal is her mum's Sunday roast. She says that her Yorkshire puddings are 'immense'.

LONDON PRIDE

AROUND AND ABOUT THE LIONHEARTED CAPITAL CITY

Home to more than eight million people, London is one of the greatest cities in the world. The capital provides a warm welcome to millions of tourists every year from the UK and overseas, all of whom flock to the city to enjoy its historic landmarks, amazing attractions and stunning sights.

London is expecting even more visitors for the 2012 Games and some of them might be lucky enough to catch a glimpse of Pride the lion, who is the official Team GB mascot. But Pride isn't the only big cat on show in the capital, so the next time you're in London keep your eyes open and you might just see these other famous lions.

TRAFALGAR SQUARE

Nelson's Column in Trafalgar Square is guarded by four huge bronze lions that sit at the base of the monument. Legend has it that the lions were made from the cannons of the French ships that were beaten by Lord Admiral Nelson at the famous Battle of Trafalgar in 1805.

LONDON ZOO

If you fancy going to see real-life lions in the flesh then London Zoo is the place to visit. The zoo is home to a family of four beautiful Asian lions, with parents Lucifer and Abi proudly living alongside their not-so-small cubs Rubi and Max. During the 2010 FIFA World Cup, the lions were given special footballs filled with tasty meat treats to celebrate the start of the tournament.

Four bronze lions guard Nelson's Column in Trafalgar Square.

Lions have long been among London Zoo's most popular exhibits.

Pride the Lion hopes to celebrate plenty of Team GB gold medals.

BUCKINGHAM PALACE

The Victoria Memorial in front of Buckingham Palace is a famous London landmark that is surrounded by four statues that are stood next to bronze lions. Other lion statues can be seen in and around the Palace too, most notably above the gates at the main entrance.

BRITISH MUSEUM

Everywhere you look in and outside the British Museum you'll find lions. There are lion statues, lion-shaped bottles, jewellery and furniture. Inside the Great Court there's a giant, 2000-year-old Turkish marble lion, but that's nothing compared to the angry-looking five-legged Temple Lion from Iraq, sculpted almost 3,000 years ago.

WESTMINSTER BRIDGE

Stood on the south bank of the River Thames, this 13-tonne, 150-year-old beast is called the Coade Stone Lion. It's made from the most waterproof stone in the world, which means that despite being old it still looks almost brand new. Originally the South Bank Lion (its other name) stood on top of the Lion Brewery but after that was bombed in the Second World War the statue was moved to Waterloo Station before arriving at its current home in 1966.

TEAM GB TARGETING GLORY IN 2012

SETTING THE

Team GB scooped an amazing 47 medals at the Beijing 2008 Olympic Games and will be aiming for even more in front of a home audience at London 2012. Check out our essential guide to the UK Olympians with medals in their sights.

IN THE POOL

Team GB won six medals, including two golds, in Beijing's spectacular Water Cube in 2008 and there are high hopes of doing even better at the Aquatics Centre in 2012. Medal hopeful Gemma Spofforth won the World Championship 100m Backstroke in 2009, and set a new world record time, while Keri-Anne Payne won a silver medal at Beijing 2008 in the gruelling Marathon Swimming 10km. Backstroke specialist Liam Tancock won gold in the 50m at the 2009 World Championships and will lead the men's challenge at the London 2012 Games.

> Lisa Dobriskey is Team GB's best medal hope in the women's 1500m.

> Gemma Spofforth set the world 100m Backstroke record in 2009; she wants gold at London 2012.

ON THE TRACK

Heptathlete Jessica Ennis missed out on the Beijing 2008 Games because of a foot injury but she's now the reigning World and European champion and desperate for success at London 2012. In the 1500m, Lisa Dobriskey is the second-fastest British woman of all time over the distance and after winning silver in the 2009 World Championships, she is hotly tipped to do well in London. Of the men, triple jumper Phillips Idowu came second at Beijing 2008 but definitely has the talent to be champion in 2012.

> Jason Kenny is continuing the great tradition of Team GB stars in Track Cycling.

IN THE VELODROME

After his sensational triple gold swoop at Beijing 2008, all eyes will be on Sir Chris Hoy when the Track Cycling gets underway but he's not the only star in the team. Youngster Jason Kenny was a key figure in the Team Sprint win at Beijing 2008 alongside Hoy and four years on he will be stronger and more experienced. New for 2012 is the women's Team Pursuit race and our talented squad of Lizzie Armitstead, Wendy Houvenaghel, Jo Rowsell and Rebecca Romero are already being talked about as possible champions.

BAR HIGH

Golden boys at Beijing 2008, Zac Purchase and Mark Hunter want to repeat at London 2012.

ON THE WATER

Team GB topped the medals table ahead of Australia in the Rowing at Beijing 2008 and Lightweight Double Sculls champions Zac Purchase and Mark Hunter are well fancied to defend their title at London 2012. Elsewhere, Double Sculls (2x) hopefuls Katherine Grainger and Anna Watkins won the 2010 World Championships and should be contenders for gold at Eton Dorney.

OUR OTHER MEDAL HOPEFULS

Super-fit triathlete Alistair Brownlee is a top tip for gold in 2012 after winning the World Championship series in 2009 and then becoming European champion in 2010 and it will be no surprise if he becomes the champion in 2012. Gymnast Beth Tweddle has been winning medals for nearly 10 years and after narrowly missing out on bronze in the Uneven Bars at Beijing 2008, she'll be desperate to add medals from an Olympic Games to her collection. In the ring, boxer Simon Vallily is the reigning Commonwealth Heavy Weight champion while Dressage rider Laura Bechtolsheimer was part of the team that won silver at the most recent World and European championships.

Alistair Brownlee is a star in one of the Olympic Games' most gruelling events, the Triathlon.

LEE PEARSON

MR DRESSAGE

The world's most successful Paralympic Dressage rider, Lee Pearson excels in the saddle as he and his horse test their combined agility and style. A champion at three Paralympic Games (at Sydney 2000, Athens 2004 and Beijing 2008), Lee was the first ever rider with a disability to be inducted into the British Horse Society's Hall of Fame. He now has his sights sets on a fourth consecutive Paralympic Games and even more medals.

' London 2012 is going to be brilliant for British sport and for British people getting into sport. I cannot wait. '

4 AMAZING FACTS

1 In 2003 he became the only rider with a disability to win a title at the British Dressage National Championships, competing against non-disabled riders.

Both horse and rider must look at their best in the Dressage event

2 Dressage can be an expensive sport if you own your own horse and in 2010 alone Lee spent £30,000, donated by a Paralympic charity, to buy a new horse called Silhouette. 'She is a phenomenal horse,' he said. 'She's really well behaved yet with so much power and rideability.'

GETTING PERSONAL

→ Lee began riding as a child because he couldn't join his two brothers when they went out on their BMXs. His parents bought him a donkey called Sally and his love affair with horses began.

→ When he's not in the saddle, Lee is a speed freak and adores fast cars. He's raced in a Ferrari and arrived for his wedding driving in a bright yellow Lamborghini.

London 2012 will be Lee's fourth Paralympic Games

3 Lee made his competitive debut in Dressage in 1998 and has now won an incredible 27 gold medals at the Paralympic Games, World Championships and European Championships. His first Paralympic Games gold medal came at Sydney 2000.

4 A rider normally trains a horse for years in preparation for a big dressage competition but Lee secured a hat-trick of Paralympic Games gold medals at Beijing 2008 on his horse, Gentleman, just eight months after first putting a saddle on him.

Gentleman had little experience, but Lee had more than enough.

BEYOND LONDON

THE 2012 GAMES ACROSS THE UK

HADLEIGH FARM

A 550-acre farm that will be an amazing venue for what's sure to be an exciting Mountain Bike competition.

LOCATION: Essex
SPORTS: Mountain Biking
DID YOU KNOW? Riders will be able to see the 700-year-old Hadleigh Castle in the background as they tear around the track.

WEYMOUTH AND PORTLAND

With some of the best water for sailing in Europe, the harbour facilities were the first to be completed for the Games.

LOCATION: Dorset
SPORTS: Sailing, Paralympic Sailing
DID YOU KNOW? In 2010 a Second World War mine was found lying on the seabed and had to be blown up by bomb disposal experts.

BRANDS HATCH

One of the world's most iconic motor racing tracks, Brands Hatch hosted the British Grand Prix between 1964 and 1986 and currently holds many international racing events.

LOCATION: Kent
SPORT: Paralympic Road Cycling
DID YOU KNOW? Formula One World Champion Nigel Mansell won his first Grand Prix at Brands Hatch in 1985.

ETON DORNEY

Just 40 minutes by train from Central London, this fantastic lake is famous for its still water and is set in a beautiful 400-acre park.

LOCATION: Buckinghamshire
SPORTS: Rowing, Canoe Sprint, Paralympic Rowing
DID YOU KNOW? More than 30,000 trees were planted in the park after the digging of the lake was finished.

CITY OF COVENTRY STADIUM

This state-of-the-art stadium is home to Coventry City Football Club and it also boasts a hotel, exhibition hall, leisure club, casino and shopping centre.

LOCATION: West Midlands
SPORT: Football
DID YOU KNOW? Pop legends Take That performed in front of 150,000 fans during three sell-out concerts at the Stadium in 2009.

LEE VALLEY WHITE WATER CENTRE

Thousands of spectators will flock to the Centre to enjoy seeing the world's best canoeists tackle two testing courses.

LOCATION: Hertfordshire
SPORT: Canoe Slalom
DID YOU KNOW? Although specially built for London 2012, the Centre is open to the public before and after the Games.

OLD TRAFFORD

Home to Manchester United Football Club, this is the biggest stadium in the Premier League and the 11th largest in Europe.

LOCATION: Manchester

SPORT: Football

DID YOU KNOW? The first football match held at Old Trafford was more than 100 years ago and was between United and their arch-rivals Liverpool.

ST JAMES'S PARK

Newcastle United's magnificent home stadium is positioned right in the middle of the city centre and its huge white roof can be seen for miles around.

LOCATION: Newcastle

SPORT: Football

DID YOU KNOW? Inside the Gallowgate End stand there's a bar called Shearer's, named after Newcastle's ex-striker and *Match of the Day* pundit Alan Shearer.

HAMPDEN PARK

The stadium is used by Scotland's national football team and for Scottish club cup finals, but it's also home to Scottish League minnows Queen's Park.

LOCATION: Glasgow

SPORT: Football

DID YOU KNOW? 149,415 fans crammed into the stadium back in 1937 to watch Scotland play England.

GO FIGURE

2,200 – Length in metres of the eight-lane rowing course at Eton Dorney

900 – Number of catering staff employed to cook and serve food inside the Millennium Stadium for every big match

30 – Seconds it would take to fill a 25-metre swimming pool by the powerful pumps at Lee Valley White Water Centre

113 – Millions of pounds to build the Coventry Stadium

233 – Kilometres between the Olympic Park and Weymouth in Dorset

MILLENNIUM STADIUM

The home of the Welsh rugby union team, it was also used to host the FA Cup final between 2001 and 2006 when Wembley Stadium was being rebuilt.

LOCATION: Cardiff

SPORT: Football

DID YOU KNOW? The Stadium is also home to a hawk called Dad – his job is to scare seagulls and pigeons off the pitch.

TOM DALEY
THE BOY WONDER

Diver Tom Daley will be one of the youngest members of Team GB but few of his teammates can match his amazing achievements. The 2009 World Champion has been winning national and international titles since he was 10 years old and will fulfil a lifelong ambition if he lands gold at the London 2012 Games.

Tom is combining his training with work on three A levels at college.

Tom has twice completed a perfect dive in a major competition.

4 AMAZING FACTS

1 At the Beijing 2008 Games, Tom was the youngest member of Team GB at the age of just 14. He did himself proud by finishing in seventh place in the 10m Platform event and eighth in the Synchronised 10m Platform competition.

2 All seven judges at a Diving Grand Prix event at Fort Lauderdale, USA, in 2009 awarded Tom the maximum score of 10 for one of his amazing, acrobatic dives. In the Dehli 2010 Commonwealth Games final, he repeated the incredible feat with another perfect dive.

3 Plymouth City Council were so thrilled at Tom's sensational display in winning the 2009 World Championships at the age of just 15 that they organised an open-top bus ride around the city to celebrate his success. Thousands of fans packed the streets to cheer their local hero as he smiled and waved his way along the parade route in front of a sea of Union Jack flags.

Diving has an age-limit low enough for Tom to compete.

4 Because of his age, up until now, Tom has been unable to try some of the world's most difficult dives, relying on perfect execution of less difficult ones to score highly with the judges. But he is practising hard on two difficult new dives he is planning to show off at the London 2012 Games.

Tom has promised to attempt riskier dives as he gets older.

> ' *It's just everyone's dream when they are a little kid, everyone wants to be an Olympian and get an Olympic gold medal.* '

GETTING PERSONAL

→ After he has retired from diving, Tom's ambition is to become a television presenter and he would love to work on *Blue Peter*.

→ Whenever he gets a break from competition, the teenager loves nothing more than going on caravan holidays with his family in Newquay, Cornwall.

GOLDEN MEMORIES

THE STORY OF THE FABULOUS SUCCESS OF PARALYMPICSGB

The performance of the 206 GB athletes at the Beijing 2008 Paralympic Games was superb. ParalympicsGB claimed an incredible 102 medals, their best haul for 20 years. The 42 gold medals meant only hosts China ended ahead of GB in the final medals table. This is the story of ParalympicsGB's brilliant Games.

Two outstanding performances have come from English cyclist Darren Kenny and Welsh swimmer David Roberts, who both won four gold medals each. Kenny won two golds at the Athens 2004 Paralympic Games but doubled that at Beijing 2008 with victory in the Pursuit, Kilo, Team Sprint and Road Race, while Roberts was simply superb in the Water Cube with wins in the 100m Freestyle, 400m Freestyle, 50m Freestyle and 4 x 100m Freestyle Relay. Roberts has now won 11 gold medals at Paralympic Games in his career – equalling Tanni-Grey Thompson's British record.

The Paralympic Cycling – Road and Track – events were a huge success for the UK and two gold medals each for Mark Bristow, Jody Cundy, Antony Kappes, Barney Storey, Aileen McGlynn, Ellen Hunter, Simon Richardson, David Stone and Sarah Storey helped ParalympicsGB finish first in the medals table ahead of the USA. In the pool, our swimmers claimed a total of 41 medals, including 11 golds. Sascha Kindred was the Men's 200m Individual Medley and 100m Breaststroke champion but the big story was the success of 13-year-old Ellie Simmonds, who made history as Great Britain's youngest ever Paralympic champion after her stunning win in the 100m Freestyle. She won gold in the 400m Freestyle too.

Elsewhere, wheelchair racer David Weir was ParalympicsGB's only gold medallist in the Paralympic Athletics after storming to victory in both the 800m and 1500m, while Wheelchair Tennis ace Peter Norfolk successfully defended his title in the Men's Quad Singles. There were also gold medals for rowers Tom Aggar and Helene Raynsford while the Paralympic Archery competition saw John Stubbs and Danielle Brown crowned champions in the men's and women's Individual Compound events.

ROLL OF HONOUR
ParalympicsGB's Beijing 2008 gold medallists

DARREN KENNY (CYCLING – TRACK AND ROAD)
Pursuit, Kilo, Team Sprint, Road Race

DAVID ROBERTS (SWIMMING)
100m Freestyle, 400m Freestyle, 50m Freestyle,
4 x 100m Freestyle Relay

LEE PEARSON (EQUESTRIAN)
Championship Test: Individual, Freestyle Test:
Individual, Team – Open

MARK BRISTOW (CYCLING – TRACK)
Kilo, Team Sprint

SOPHIE CHRISTIANSEN (EQUESTRIAN)
Championship Test: Individual, Team Dressage

JODY CUNDY (CYCLING – TRACK)
Kilo, Team Sprint

ANNE DUNHAM (EQUESTRIAN)
Championship Test: Individual, Team Dressage

**ANTHONY KAPPES, BARNEY STOREY
(CYCLING – TRACK)**
Kilo, Sprint

SASCHA KINDRED (SWIMMING)
200m Individual Medley, 100m Breaststroke

**AILEEN MCGLYNN, ELLEN HUNTER
(CYCLING – TRACK)**
Individual Pursuit, Kilo

SIMON RICHARDSON (CYCLING – TRACK)
Individual Pursuit, Kilo

ELLIE SIMMONDS (SWIMMING)
100m Freestyle, 400m Freestyle

DAVID STONE (CYCLING – ROAD)
Time Trial, Mixed Individual Road Race

SARAH STOREY (CYCLING – TRACK AND ROAD)
Individual Pursuit, Time Trial

DAVID WEIR (ATHLETICS)
800m, 1500m

TOM AGGAR (ROWING)
Single Sculls

DANIELLE BROWN (ARCHERY)
Individual Compound

HEATHER FREDERIKSEN (SWIMMING)
100m Backstroke

RACHEL MORRIS (CYCLING – ROAD)
Time Trial

**DAN BENTLEY, DAVID SMITH, ZOE ROBINSON,
NIGEL MURRAY (BOCCIA)**
Mixed Team

GRAHAM EDMUNDS (SWIMMING)
4 x 100m Freestyle Relay

SAM HYND (SWIMMING)
400m Freestyle

LIZ JOHNSON (SWIMMING)
100m Breaststroke

SIMON LAURENS (EQUESTRIAN)
Championship Test: Individual

PETER NORFOLK (TENNIS)
Quad Singles

HELENE RAYNSFORD (ROWING)
Single Sculls

MATT SKELHON (SHOOTING)
R3 10km Air Rifle Prone

JOHN STUBBS (ARCHERY)
Individual Compound

MATT WALKER (SWIMMING)
4 x 100m Freestyle Relay

ROBERT WELBOURN (SWIMMING)
4 x 100m Freestyle Relay

ParalympicsGB athletes enjoyed golden moments in numerous sports at the Beijing 2008 Paralympic Games. Here are possibly six of the best:
(Opposite left) archer Danielle Brown.
(Opposite right) cyclist Darren Kenny.
(Top) swimmer Sascha Kindred.
(Upper middle) athlete David Weir.
(Lower middle) swimmer Ellie Simmonds.
(Right) swimmer David Roberts

LONDON 1948

STORY OF THE LONDON 1948 OLYMPIC GAMES

The London 2012 Olympic Games will be the third time the city had hosted the famous Games, 64 years after the world's finest athletes last gathered together here to compete for a precious gold medal. In 1948 more than 4,000 men and women, from a then record 59 different countries, travelled to London for the Games – the first since Berlin 1936 because of the Second World War – and, for the first time ever, the Games were shown on television. This is the story of the London 1948 Olympic Games.

GOLDEN GREATS

Great Britain won three gold medals at the London 1948 Games and all three were connected with water. Stewart Morris and David Bond teamed up together to win the Swallow Class in the Sailing while Jack Wilson and Ran Laurie were the champions of the Coxless Pairs in the Rowing. The third goal medal also came in the Rowing when Dickie Burnell and Bert Bushnell were fastest in the Double Sculls.

Sailors David Bond (left) and Stewart Morris won London 1948 gold medals in Torquay.

THE GAMES IN NUMBERS

11 – The height in metres of the flagpole used to fly the Olympic Flag at Wembley Stadium

14 – Number of countries, including India and Pakistan, competing for the first time

59 – Number of different countries that sent athletes to the Games

390 – Number of women athletes who competed in London, compared to 3,714 men

1,000 – Pounds the BBC paid to broadcast the Games on television

2,500 – Number of pigeons released during the Opening Ceremony

85,000 – Number of people who were packed into Wembley Stadium for the Opening Ceremony

THE AUSTERITY GAMES

Even though they were a big success, the 1948 Olympic Games were called the Austerity Games because it was three years after the end of the Second World War and the country did not have much money to spend. That meant there was no specially built Olympic Village and the 4,000 athletes were housed in schools, nurses' hostels and RAF bases. The athletes had to bring their own towels and were transported to their events by London buses. The greyhound race track at Wembley Stadium was dug up for two weeks before the Games began and resurfaced for the Athletics events and when the Empire Pool at Wembley Arena was not in use, it was covered up with a massive platform so that the Olympic Boxing events could be staged there. There were no floodlights at the Olympic Velodrome and on one evening car headlights had to be used to finish the day's racing.

Maureen Gardner (far right) won her 80m Hurdles heat, but lost the Final in a photo-finish.

GIRL POWER

Team GB may have narrowly missed out on gold on the track but our women athletes were still in great form in 1948, claiming four silver medals inside Wembley Stadium. The first came with Dorothy Manley in the 100m and two days later Maureen Gardner, a 19-year-old ballet dancer from Oxford, was second in the 80m Hurdles. Audrey Williamson, 21, also claimed a silver after finishing second to the legendary Dutchwoman Fanny Blankers-Koen in the final of the 200m and the following day Dorothy Tyler, who had competed in the Berlin 1936 Games, was second in the High Jump.

Team GB (black shorts) beat the Netherlands, but lost in the Football bronze medal play-off.

TEAM GB'S 1948 MEDAL HAUL

GOLD
DICKIE BURNELL AND **BERT BUSHNELL** (Rowing)
Double Sculls
JACK WILSON AND **RAN LAURIE** (Rowing)
Coxless Pairs
STEWART MORRIS AND **DAVID BOND** (Sailing)
Swallow Class

SILVER
THOMAS RICHARDS (Athletics)
Marathon
DOROTHY MANLEY (Athletics)
100m
AUDREY WILLIAMSON (Athletics)
200m
MAUREEN GARDNER (Athletics)
80m Hurdles
ALASTAIR McCORQUODALE, JOHN GREGORY, KENNETH JONES AND **JACK ARCHER** (Athletics)
4 x 100m Relay
DOROTHY TYLER (Athletics)
High Jump
JOHN WRIGHT (Boxing)
Middle Weight
DONALD SCOTT (Boxing)
Light Heavy Weight
ROBERT MAITLAND, IAN SCOTT AND **GORDON THOMAS** (Cycling)
Team Road Race
REG HARRIS (Cycling)
Sprint
ALAN BANNISTER AND **REG HARRIS** (Cycling)
2km Tandem
JULIAN CREUS (Weightlifting)
56kg
TEAM (Hockey)
Men's
TEAM (Rowing)
Men's Eight with Cox
TEAM (Lacrosse*)
Men's

BRONZE
TEBBS LLOYD-JOHNSON (Athletics)
50km Walk
TOMMY GODWIN (Cycling)
1km Time Trial
HARRY LLWELLYN, HENRY NICOLL AND **ARTHUR CARR** (Equestrian)
Team Jumping
CATHERINE GIBSON (Swimming)
400m Freestyle
WILFRED WATERS, ALAN GELDARD, TOMMY GODWIN AND **DAVID RICKETTS** (Cycling)
Team Pursuit
JAMES HALLIDAY (Weightlifting)
67.5kg

* As Lacrosse was an exhibition event Team GB's silver medal was unofficial.

THE FINAL COUNTDOWN

THE LAST SIX MONTHS

London has been getting ready for the Games since 2005 when it was announced that the English capital had been chosen as the host city of the 2012 Olympic Games. The last six months of preparation will be the busiest as organisers put the finishing touches in place. Take a look at what will be happening in 2012 as the start of the London 2012 Games gets closer and closer.

PASSING THE FLAME

The famous Olympic Torch Relay is a tradition of the Olympic Games and there will be a 70-day Relay around the UK before the start of the 2012 Games. The Torch will be lit in Greece – the home of the modern Olympic Games – and it will arrive in the UK in May. After that, 8,000 specially chosen Torchbearers will carry the Torch up and down the UK before it is finally carried into the Olympic Stadium on 27 July for the start of the Games.

WATCHING THE ACTION

Tickets for the London 2012 Olympic Games went on sale in March 2011, for the Paralympic Games it was September. There are 8.8 million tickets for the Olympic Games and two million for the Paralympic Games. The good news is that tickets will remain on sale until the start of every event, even if it is not a sell-out. You could also check out the free events, which include Road Cycling, Triathlon and Marathon. They won't cost you a penny and the atmosphere will be brilliant.

THE VOLUNTEERS

The London 2012 Olympic Games will see 70,000 people volunteering to help make the Games run as smoothly as possible. A day's volunteering will last eight hours and all applicants have agreed to work for at least 10 days either at the Olympic or Paralympic Games. Before the Games they will be trained to make sure they are ready for Britain's biggest ever sports party.

TESTING THE VENUES

It's important that all the venues are ready for the Games and 2012 will see many of the sites hosting warm-up events. In February, the Velodrome will be the venue for the UCI Track Cycling World Cup Classic and in March the Aquatics Centre will be the place to watch the British Swimming Championships. The first athletics event to be staged at the showpiece Olympic Stadium will be in May, the British Universities and Colleges Sport Championships.

SELECTING THE ATHLETES

Every UK athlete dreaming of going to the London 2012 Games has to earn the chance to compete and 2012 will see many of the sports holding trials to select our medal hopefuls. For example, our swimmers will all be in action in March in the new £268-million Aquatics Centre as they battle to qualify while many of our athletes will have to wait until June for their chance to win a place in the team.

BEYOND SPORT

A month before the start of the Games the London 2012 Festival will be held in the capital – an unmissable chance to celebrate the Games through dance, music, theatre, the visual arts and film. Artists, musicians and performers from across the UK and the world will be invited to London to take part and there will be more than 1,000 events and an estimated audience of more than three million people. The Festival begins on 21 June and ends on 9 September – the final day of the 2012 Paralympics.

BETH TWEDDLE

GOLDEN GYMNAST

Britain's most successful ever gymnast, Beth Tweddle has been one of the sport's finest competitors for 10 years and boasts a great collection of medals – 19 (nine gold) at major competitions. After missing out on a medal at Beijing 2008, she's desperate for glory in front of her home fans at London 2012.

4 AMAZING FACTS

1 Beth made headlines in 2006 when she went to Denmark to compete in Uneven Bars in the World Championships. Britain had never won a gold medal in the competition but just one day after a nasty fall, she beat the defending champion Anastasia Liukin to take the title and make history.

Beth was Britain's first-ever World Champion in a Gymnastics event

2 Beth is as brave as she is graceful and athletic. In 2002 she delayed a planned operation on an injured shoulder so she could compete at the Manchester 2002 Commonwealth Games. It proved a wise move as she won one gold and two silver medals.

Spectacular dismounts from the Uneven Bars are Beth's specialities

3 The European Championships that were staged in 2010 in Birmingham were the most successful of Beth's career so far as she won gold in both the Uneven Bars and Floor Exercise, as well as a silver medal in the Team event.

Beth has tasted victory in the World and European Championships ...

4 Beth has competed at the Olympic Games twice. Her first appearance was at Athens 2004. Then, at the Beijing 2008 Games, she came very close to winning a medal after finishing fourth in the Uneven Bars.

... all that remains for Beth is Olympic glory at London 2012

BORN: 1 April 1985 (Johannesburg, South Africa)

EDUCATED: Queens School (Chester), Liverpool John Moores University

CLUB: City Of Liverpool

CAREER HIGHLIGHTS: 2002 Commonwealth Uneven Bars champion, 2006 World Uneven Bars champion, 2006 European Uneven Bars champion, 2009 European Uneven Bars and Floor champion, 2009 World Floor Exercise champion, 2010 European Uneven Bars and Floor Exercise champion, 2010 World Uneven Bars champion, 2011 European Uneven Bars champion

" Everyone keeps telling me how old I am but my motivation is still there and the main motivation is competing at London 2012."

GETTING PERSONAL

➡ Beth represents the UK but she was born and, as a baby, lived in Johannesburg because her dad was working in South Africa. The family returned to England when she was 18 months old.

➡ She's a big football fan and after studying in the city she became a dedicated Liverpool supporter.

➡ Beth began her gymnastics career at the age of seven when she joined the Crewe and Nantwich club. Aged 13 she spent four days in hospital after undergoing an operation to mend an ankle she had fractured in training.

PARALYMPIC GAMES

UK STARS WITH MEDALS IN THEIR SIGHTS

ParalympicsGB took the Beijing 2008 Paralympic Games by storm, collecting 102 medals including 42 golds. That great performance earned the team second place in the final medals table behind hosts China and they'll be hoping to do even better on home soil. These UK Paralympians are aiming for glory in 2012.

PARALYMPIC ATHLETICS

Wheelchair racing legend David Weir won two gold medals at the Beijing 2008 Paralympic Games and he's hot favourite to dominate again in the 800m and 1500m. Two other names to watch out for inside the Olympic Stadium are 100m sprint sensation Libby Clegg and teenage wheelchair racer Jade Jones, who won five gold medals in the World Junior Championships in the Czech Republic in 2010.

Wheelchair race ace David Weir competes at every distance from 100m to the Marathon.

PARALYMPIC CYCLING

Veteran Darren Kenny won four gold medals on the road and in the Velodrome at Beijing 2008 but he's aiming for five in London. Kenny's teammate Jody Cundy is another speed machine who holds the world record for the 200m Sprint, while swimmer-turned-cyclist Sarah Storey is a strong contender to repeat her double gold medal success of 2008.

Darren Kenny will be 42 and racing in his third Paralympic Games at London 2012.

PARALYMPIC EQUESTRIAN

Team GB has a great record in the Paralympic Equestrian events and won 10 medals at Beijing 2008. Nine-time gold medallist Lee Pearson remains a legend of the sport and will be desperate to add to his tally on home soil, while female stars Sophie Christiansen and Emma Sheardown both hold high hopes of winning medals.

Sophie Christiansen, riding Lambrusco III, has gold medal dreams in the Dressage.

Ellie Simmonds produced an amazing sprint finish to win the 100m Freestyle.

PARALYMPIC SWIMMING

Ellie Simmonds was just 13 when she won an astonishing two gold medals at Beijing 2008 and hopes are high that the brilliant freestyler will bag more titles in home water. World record holder Jonathan Fox is the man everyone has to beat in the 100m Backstroke, while Liz Johnson is another star to keep your eye on because she's the reigning 100m Breaststroke champion.

Tom Aggar is one of the men to watch in the London 2012 Paralympic Rowing events.

BEST OF THE REST

Tom Aggar is widely expected to storm to Paralympic Rowing gold having dominated the Single Sculls events over the last four years, while sensational young archer Danielle Brown will be hoping to follow up her gold at Beijing 2008 with another win in London. Also watch out for Boccia, a sport similar to bowls, where Nigel Murray is number one in the world.

STOKE MANDEVILLE HOSPITAL

➡ Although the first official Paralympic Games were held in Rome in 1960, it was during the London 1948 Olympic Games that a first competition for disabled athletes was held. Called the Stoke Mandeville Games and held at the local hospital, the competition was originally organised for 16 British soldiers who had suffered back injuries in the Second World War, but in 1952 they were joined by veterans from Holland to make it an international event. Eight years later, the Paralympic Games were born in Italy and in 1984 the Games returned to Stoke Mandeville when the hospital was a joint host with New York in the United States. However, it was at Seoul 1988 that the event was first held under the title of the Paralympic Games.

MEET THE COACHES

THE PEOPLE BEHIND PARALYMPICSGB'S STARS

THE BIG BOSS

NAME PENNY BRISCOE
TITLE PERFORMANCE DIRECTOR,
BRITISH PARALYMPIC ASSOCIATION

■ Overall responsibility for ParalympicsGB's success in London lies with this former national canoeing coach, who has worked tirelessly to ensure that all our athletes are ready to produce their very best performances during the 11 days of the 2012 Paralympic Games.

■ She makes sure everyone has the right equipment, best facilities and easiest travel arrangements, so the athletes have more time to concentrate on their sports. She's also set them performance targets, reviewed every three months, to ensure the athletes stay on top.

➡ **Use the best training facilities**

➡ **Set regular performance targets**

THE CYCLING CHIEF

NAME CHRIS FURBER
TITLE LEAD COACH, GB PARA-CYCLING SQUAD

■ It won't be easy to match the amazing 17 gold medals won by the UK's cyclists at the Beijing 2008 Paralympic Games but if anyone can guide them to glory for a second time, it's Chris Furber. He has steered Team GB to more than 60 gold medals at the Paralympic Games and Para-Cycling World Championships since taking charge of the squad in 2006.

■ Before becoming lead coach, Furber was a talent coach for British Cycling and helped to develop the careers of future stars like Jason Kenny and Shanaze Reade.

➡ **Experiment with new ideas**

➡ **Push an extra 1 per cent in training every day**

Winning gold medals is not easy. Champions need talent, dedication, determination and the ability to produce their very best performances under pressure. They also need one other vital ingredient to make it on to the podium – a brilliant coach. Luckily for ParalympicsGB, nothing has been left to chance as they look to improve on their superb haul of 102 medals at the Beijing 2008 Paralympic Games. Over £50 million has been spent supporting the athletes since then and more than 50 professional coaches have been employed to work alongside them.

THE TRACK GURU

NAME PETER ERIKSSON

TITLE HEAD COACH, UK ATHLETICS PARALYMPIC PROGRAMME

■ This Swedish legend is the most successful Athletics coach in Paralympic Games history. So far in his brilliant career he has helped his athletes to win a total of 119 medals. He has coached athletes from 10 different countries but since 2008 his training skills have been exclusively used by ParalympicsGB and, as expected, great improvements have been made.

→ **Study what you do wrong and put it right**

→ **Push yourself to the limit physically and mentally**

THE POOL EXPERT

NAME JOHN ATKINSON

TITLE NATIONAL PERFORMANCE DIRECTOR, BRITISH DISABILITY SWIMMING

■ After working in Australia for a number of years, the British-born swimming coach returned to the UK in 2001 and has been helping to develop our best talent in the pool ever since. As team leader, it's been his job to ensure that all the swimmers and their individual coaches have followed the right training plans in the lead up to the Games.

→ **Keep track of every performance in the pool and build on each effort**

→ **Drive each other on by creating a great team spirit**

PUZZLE IT OUT

MEGA WORDSEARCH

Can you find the 20 Olympic and Paralympic sports hiding in the grid below?

ARCHERY	DIVING	HOCKEY	SHOOTING
ATHLETICS	EQUESTRIAN	JUDO	SWIMMING
BADMINTON	FENCING	MODERN	WHEELCHAIR
BOCCIA	FOOTBALL	PENTATHLON	RUGBY
BOXING	GOALBALL	POWERLIFTING	
BMX CYCLING	HANDBALL	ROWING	

```
R O W Y G A M E Q U E S T R I A N A S T
I K S O V N O S I K F U V O S B I N T R
W S H A N D B A L L A P L A T D F D O A
H C O L D O U E A A R P T P Y O B A R L
E L O L R U Y F T N R H Y E O T Y D M L
E A T B U G A E H O L N A T B I T E O D
L E I A M Q P N G E D D B R O P J U D O
C U N D O U U C T G A A W I C K S Y E G
H W G M O K N I J H L T O F C A F Y R H
A T H I T C C N X L S H T I I R U R N I
I P A N I S P G O L E O F D A V G E P J
R A R T R A O Z L I U R I W C E G H E G
R U X O A B H A I S Q I O H O U I C N N
U Q M N R N B O X I N G A W Q D T R T I
G I B A L L I M B A S X X A I C S A A L
B O A X A O W X L T A Y R Z P N A R T C
Y N I O L A T F O M E E M N C J G U H Y
O A G C R P O W E R L I F T I N G E L C
L E W I Y G N I M M I W S W L A L A O X
Y E K C O H N A R J D J I O A C E J N M
M I C A E Y I G N I V I D K N L E H F B
```

PARALYMPIC WORDFIT

Can you fit the 15 ParalympicsGB stars listed below into the grid on the right?

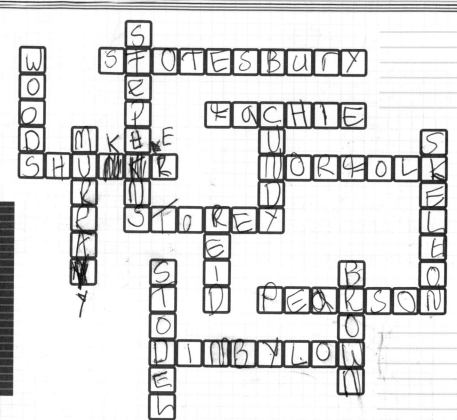

LONDON 2012 CROSSWORD

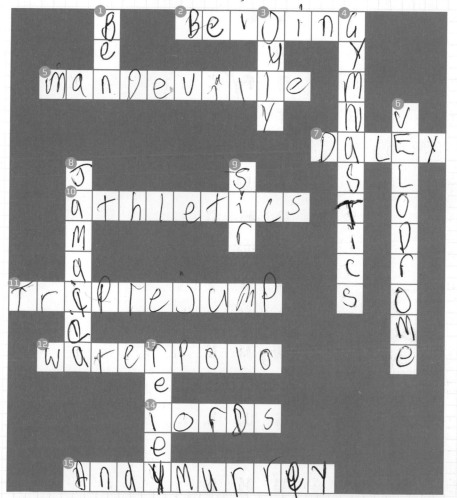

ACROSS

2 The city that hosted the 2008 Games in China (7)

5 One of the friendly mascots for the London 2012 Games (10)

7 Surname of Team GB's brilliant teenage diving star (5)

10 The main sport that will take place inside the Olympic Stadium (9)

11 Phillips Idowu will be going for gold in this event (6, 4)

12 A team sport played in the swimming pool using a ball (5, 4)

14 Famous cricket ground that will be the venue for Archery at the London 2012 Games (5)

15 Team GB's best tennis player (4, 6)

DOWN

1 First name of Team GB's triple gold medal winning sailor (3)

3 The month in which the London 2012 Olympic Games begins (4)

4 The indoor sport that stars Team GB's Beth Tweddle (10)

6 Team GB's cyclists will be whizzing around the track in this venue (9)

8 The country that Usain Bolt runs for (7)

9 The title given to Chris Hoy when he was knighted by Her Majesty the Queen (3)

13 A race around the athletics track where runners pass on a baton (5)

SAILOR SUPREME BEN AINSLIE

With three gold medals and a silver to his name, Ben Ainslie is already an Olympic legend, but he still has his sights firmly set on winning an incredible fourth gold at the London 2012 Olympic Games. The competition will be the toughest of his career, but few would bet against him making history in the seas off Weymouth and Portland.

To compete at Olympic standard, Ben has to build himself up.

ATHENS 2004 GBR

4 AMAZING FACTS

1 You need to be incredibly strong to handle the Finn class boats that Ben sails and as a result he has had to put on 15 kilograms of muscle to be able to compete. His secret to gaining the extra muscle is to eat as much steak as he possibly can in between visits to the gym.

2 Her Majesty the Queen has recognised Ben's achievements on three separate occasions, awarding him an MBE in 2001, an OBE four years later and after his third gold medal he was made a CBE, which stands for Commander of the Order of the British Empire.

Ben has been winning international competitions for almost 20 years.

3 Watched on TV by millions of fans in 183 countries around the world, Ben proved he is still one of the best all-round sailors by winning the 2010 World Match Racing Tour, a nine-race event featuring many of the world's greatest sailors.

Ben's dad skippered a yacht in the first Round the World Race in 1973–74.

4 The highlight of Ben's career was winning gold in the Laser class at the Sydney 2000 Games when he beat Brazilian legend Robert Scheidt in one of the most dramatic battles ever seen in the history of the Games. Knowing that his rival would be crowned champion if he finished 21st or better in the final race, Ben deliberately slowed down so that he could protect 21st position from Scheidt and in a masterclass of boat handling, Ben's tactics worked perfectly.

Ben's Laser class gold medal at the Sydney 2000 Games was an amazing victory.

GETTING PERSONAL

➡ When he's relaxing before a big race, Ben likes to listen to music from bands such as Snow Patrol and The Killers.

➡ When's he's not in a boat, Ben loves playing and watching football and supports Chelsea.

➡ If he hadn't become a professional sailor, Ben says he would have tried to become a Formula One racing driver.

FACT FILE

BORN: 5 February 1977 (Macclesfield, Cheshire)
EDUCATED: Peter Symonds College (Winchester), Truro School (Cornwall)
CLUBS: Honorary member Royal Lymington and Royal Cornwall Yacht Club and Restronquet Sailing Club
CAREER HIGHLIGHTS: 2004 and 2008 Olympic champion (Finn); 2000 Olympic champion (Laser); 1996 Olympic silver medallist (Laser); 1998, 2002 and 2008 World Sailor of the Year; 2010 World Match Racing Tour champion

Ben hopes to be the first British sailor to win gold at four Olympic Games.

'In any Olympics there are one or two people who stand out. I certainly think I can be one of those people. It would be big deal for me personally to win a fourth gold.'

TERRIFIC TRIVIA QUIZ

Answer as many of these questions as you can and see how many points you can score.

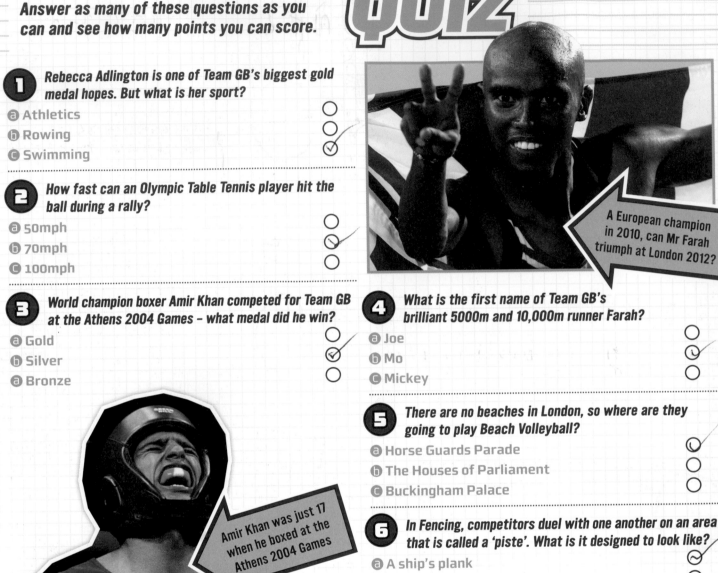

A European champion in 2010, can Mr Farah triumph at London 2012?

1 Rebecca Adlington is one of Team GB's biggest gold medal hopes. But what is her sport?
a Athletics ○
b Rowing ○
c Swimming ✓

2 How fast can an Olympic Table Tennis player hit the ball during a rally?
a 50mph ○
b 70mph ✓
c 100mph ○

3 World champion boxer Amir Khan competed for Team GB at the Athens 2004 Games – what medal did he win?
a Gold ○
b Silver ✓
a Bronze ○

Amir Khan was just 17 when he boxed at the Athens 2004 Games

4 What is the first name of Team GB's brilliant 5000m and 10,000m runner Farah?
a Joe ○
b Mo ✓
c Mickey ○

5 There are no beaches in London, so where are they going to play Beach Volleyball?
a Horse Guards Parade ✓
b The Houses of Parliament ○
c Buckingham Palace ○

6 In Fencing, competitors duel with one another on an area that is called a 'piste'. What is it designed to look like?
a A ship's plank ✓
b A castle's hallway ○
c A railway track ○

7 How many tickets will be on sale for the London 2012 Olympic Games and Paralympic Games?
a 1 million ○
b 5 million ○
c 10.8 million ✓

8 How many gold medals did Team GB win at the Beijing 2008 Games?
a 9 ○
b 14 ✓
c 19 ✓

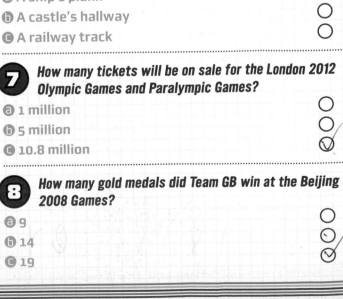

9 Great Britain's Steph Twell is tipped to do well in which Athletics event?

ⓐ 1500m ◯
ⓑ 100m Hurdles ◯
ⓒ Marathon ◉

10 How many friendship bracelets does Olympic mascot Wenlock wear on his wrists?

ⓐ 1 ◯
ⓑ 2 ◯
ⓒ 5 ◉

11 Which one of these three stadiums will be used for Football matches at the London 2012 Games?

ⓐ Craven Cottage ◯
ⓑ Old Trafford ◯
ⓒ Stamford Bridge ◉

12 What's the name of the exciting fast-paced Paralympic sport where spectators get to see, on average, more than four shots per minute during the action?

ⓐ Goalball ◯
ⓑ Softball ◯
ⓒ Handball ◉

13 Bradley Wiggins has won gold at the last two Olympic Games – but in which sport?

ⓐ Judo ◯
ⓑ Track Cycling ◯
ⓒ Sailing ◉

14 The London 2012 Games begin on 27 July 2012 and will last for how many days?

ⓐ 16 ◯
ⓑ 12 ◯
ⓒ 25 ◉

15 Where did the Opening Ceremony of the 1948 London Olympic Games take place?

ⓐ White City Stadium ◯
ⓑ Wembley Stadium ◉
ⓒ Crystal Palace ◯

Steph Twell became the world junior champion in July 2008.

The centrepiece of the London 2012 Games is the Olympic Stadium

16 Runner Stefanie Reid switched from which country to compete for ParalympicsGB at the 2012 Games?

ⓐ Canada ◯
ⓑ France ◯
ⓒ Australia ◉

17 Team GB Basketball star Luol Deng plays for which NBA team?

ⓐ Los Angeles Lakers ◯
ⓑ New York Knicks ◉
ⓒ Chicago Bulls ◯

18 Which of these is NOT a sport at the Olympic Games?

ⓐ Wrestling ◯
ⓑ Darts ◉
ⓒ Table Tennis ◯

19 A special high-speed train service will run between Kent and London during the 2012 Games. What is its name?

ⓐ The Javelin® ◯
ⓑ The Torch® ◉
ⓒ The Discus® ◯

Fans will be able to travel to London at high speed and in great comfort

20 Which city has been chosen to host the 2016 Olympic and Paralympic Games?

ⓐ New York ◯
ⓑ Tokyo ◯
ⓒ Rio de Janeiro ◉

SCORE BOARD
Answers on page 62
2 POINTS for each correct answer

MY SCORE ◯ **OUT OF 40**

SARAH STOREY

FROM POOL TO BIKE

Sarah Storey loves a challenge. In 2005, after winning a stunning 16 Paralympic Swimming medals (five gold), she took up Cycling (Track and Road). At Beijing 2008 she added two Cycling gold medals to her collection. In 2010 she became the first cyclist with a disability to ride for England at the Commonwealth Games. Now she's after more glory in 2012!

4 AMAZING FACTS

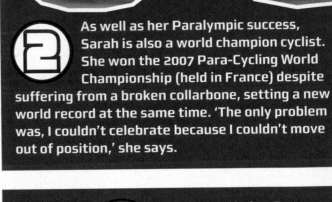

Sarah was prepared to ride through the pain barrier to win medals

1 Sarah started swimming seriously at the age of 10 and just four years later she was selected for ParalympicsGB to compete at the Barcelona 1992 Paralympic Games. No one had heard of her before the competition but they certainly knew who she was by the end of it. She won two gold medals in the pool, breaking two world records in the process.

2 As well as her Paralympic success, Sarah is also a world champion cyclist. She won the 2007 Para-Cycling World Championship (held in France) despite suffering from a broken collarbone, setting a new world record at the same time. 'The only problem was, I couldn't celebrate because I couldn't move out of position,' she says.

London 2012 will come 20 years after Sarah's first Paralympic Games

4 She is married to Barney Storey, who won two Paralympic Cycling gold medals at the Beijing 2008 Games. Barney is a pilot rider for blind/visually impaired cyclists in the tandem track events.

3 Sarah swapped swimming for cycling in 2005 because of an ear infection. It meant she wasn't allowed in the pool and she started training on a bike to keep fit. Once she decided her swimming days were over, she hasn't looked back.

Sarah chases Paralympics glory with almost unparalleled dedication

GETTING PERSONAL

➡ Sarah was always a sporting star at school. 'When I was a kid I used to do every sport going,' she says. 'I was on the boys' cricket team, I played on the county netball team. I was the county table tennis champion, I ran for the county and swimming was the first sport that chose me at international level.'

➡ Sarah and Barney are patrons of the Children's Adventure Farm Trust. It's a charity based in an old farm in Cheshire that offers sporting activities for children with severe disabilities.

➡ Her teammates call her 'Motorbike' because she 'leads from the front and rips it up'.

❝ When I was six years old, I was watching the Olympics and I said then I wanted to go when I was fourteen. ❞

FACT FILE

BORN: 26 October 1977 (Manchester)
EDUCATED: Leeds University
CLUB: Horizon Fitness
CAREER HIGHLIGHTS:
SWIMMING: 1992 Paralympic 100m Backstroke champion, 1992 Paralympic 200m Individual Medley champion, 1996 Paralympic 100m Backstroke champion, 1996 Paralympic 100m Breaststroke champion, 1996 Paralympic 200m Individual Medley champion.
CYCLING: 2008 Paralympic Time Trial champion, 2008 Paralympic Individual Pursuit champion

TEAM GB PICTURE QUIZ

Answer as many of these questions as you can and see how many points you can score.

MATCH THE RACE

Which track events do these five Team GB stars compete in?

ⓐ 800m ○   ⓑ 400m ○   ⓒ 400m ○ Hurdles   ⓓ 1500m ○   ⓔ 110m ○ Hurdles

① CHRISTINE OHURUOGU   ② DAVID GREENE   ③ JENNIFER MEADOWS   ④ LISA DOBRISKEY   ⑤ ANDY TURNER

WHAT HAPPENS WHERE?

Here are five Olympic venues – can you tell us what sport is played at each one?

❶ Tennis ©
❷ Swimming Ⓑ
❸ Rowing Ⓐ
❹ Basketball Ⓒ
❺ Cycling Ⓓ

BOXING LEGENDS

These three boxers won Olympic medals for Team GB. Can you indentify them?

❶ Audley Harrison Ⓑ

❷ James DeGale Ⓒ

❸ Amir Khan Ⓐ

WHEELS OR WATER?

Do these female Team GB stars ride a bike or swim in the pool? 15 easy points up for grabs!

ⓐ Victoria Pendleton
  SWIM ◯ BIKE ✓

ⓑ Fran Halsall
  SWIM ✓ BIKE ◯

ⓒ Shanaze Reade
  SWIM ◯ BIKE ✓

ⓓ Rebecca Romero
  SWIM ◯ BIKE ✓

ⓔ Gemma Spofforth
  SWIM ✓ BIKE ◯

OLD SKOOL!

ⓐ Who is this Team GB gold medal heroine from the Athens 2004 Games?

ⓑ In which event did she not win a gold medal:
1. 400m Hurdles ✓   2. 1500m ◯   3. 800m

SCORE BOARD

Answers on page 62

3 POINTS for each correct answer

MY SCORE ◯ **OUT OF 60**

ANSWERS

1. c	6. b	11. b	16. a
2. c	7. c	12. a	17. c
3. b	8. c	13. b	18. b
4. b	9. a	14. a	19. a
5. a	10. c	15. b	20. c

MATCH THE RACE

1. b 400m
2. c 400m Hurdles
3. a 800m
4. d 1500m
5. e 110m Hurdles

WHAT HAPPENS WHERE?

1. e (Wimbledon)
2. c (Aquatics Centre)
3. a (Eton Dorney)
4. b (North Greenwich Arena)
5. d (Velodrome)

BOXING LEGENDS

1. b
2. c
3. a

WHEELS OR WATER

a. Bike
b. Swim
c. Bike
d. Bike
e. Swim

OLD SKOOL

a. Kelly Holmes
b. 400m Hurdles

ACROSS

2 Beijing
5 Mandeville
7 Daley
10 Athletics
11 Triple jump
12 Water polo
14 Lord's
15 Andy Murray

DOWN

1 Ben
3 July
4 Gymnastics
6 Velodrome
8 Jamaica
9 Sir
13 Relay

MEGA WORDSEARCH

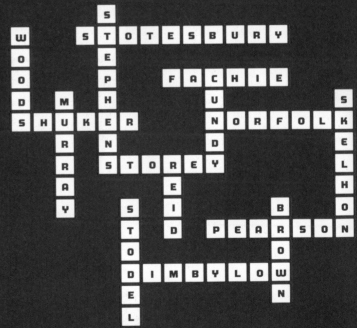